ROMANY HERBAL REMEDIES

BY GIPSY PETULENGRO

ROMANY HINTS FOR HIKERS
A ROMANY LIFE

ROMANY HERBAL REMEDIES

by

GIPSY PETULENGRO

NEWCASTLE PUBLISHING CO., INC.

NORTH HOLLYWOOD, CALIFORNIA

1982

This book was first published February 28th 1935

A Newcastle Book Reprinted By
Arrangement with Methuen & Co., Ltd.

ISBN 0-87877-016-X
First Printing August 1972
Second Printing January 1982
Printed in the United States

INTRODUCTION TO THE NEWCASTLE EDITION
GYPSIES: THE ETERNAL TRAVELERS

by
Walter Starkie, Litt.D.

There are over five mil!:on Gypsies wandering about the world today, and they have been rubbing shoulders with the peoples of the world for the past five centuries. They are still as mysterious as when they entered Europe in the fifteenth century. Sprung from Dravidian stock in the Northwest of India, they were pariahs, and according to tradition, metal-workers, minstrels, story-tellers and fakirs. They spoke a language which was derived from Sanskrit, and we find them mentioned in the eleventh century in the *Shah Nameh,* or *Book of the Kings,* by Persia's most famous poet, Firdausi (935-1020), who calls them *Luris,* the name by which they are known today in Iran. From Persia the Gypsies wandered on to Armenia, and from there into Syria and the Byzantine Empire.

The researches of the German scholars Grellmann, Pott, and Mikloyich firmly established the Gypsies' Indian origin and their migration to Europe. It was concluded that all the Gypsies belonged to the same stock, and they must have lived for a considerable time in the Greek and Slavic-speaking lands before moving on their long trek westward.

When the Original Band of Gypsies (called the "Great Band", though their number must not have exceeded five hundred), moved from Greece toward the West in 1417, they came as pilgrims with scrip and staff, declaring that they were on a pilgrimage of expiation, and called themselves Egyptians. This was definitely the first great hoax played by the Gypsies on the gullible *gorgios*.[1] They were, indeed, a band of raggle-taggle wanderers, but their leaders, who rode caparisoned horses and were well-dressed, called themselves Dukes and Earls of Little Egypt, and told the mayors and authorities of the cities that, as Egyptians, they were under a curse because they had illtreated the Holy Family when the latter had fled for refuge into Egypt from the wrath of Herod, who had massacred the Innocents. Furthermore, they added that they were under a curse as metal-workers, because they had forged the nails of the cross which had crucified Our Lord, and consequently were expiatory penitents on a pilgrimage for seven years. As a result, they were hospitably received by the city authorities everywhere, lodged in the Town Hall, and given food and money because it was regarded as an obligation to assist penitents. In addition, the King of Hungary, Sigismund (later Holy Roman Emperor), gave the Gypsies a passport, which enabled them to cross the frontiers from one country to another, and they were told by the Emperor to proceed to Rome and the Holy Father on their pilgrimage of expiation.

And so they advanced from one country to another on their wanderings toward the West. Their Dukes and Earls made treaties with some of the Kings of Europe, and so established themselves in the various countries; and later on they wandered beyond the seas through North and South America. In the eighteenth century we find them being press-ganged into the British army from England and Scotland, and fighting in the American War of Independence. We may still find members of their descendants in North and South America.

How is it possible for the Gypsies, with their ancient tribal system and their tradition of wandering slowly as nomads, to resist the overwhelming pressure of modern life? I have watched them for the past sixty years, and I have tried to sum up my conclusions after seeing them at close quarters in many countries East and West.

New Wine in old Bottles

The Gypsies are an Indian race with only two possessions: a language—Romani—and a musical scale. Their language is a close bond between them, for it enables them to communicate among themselves without being understood by the hated stranger, whom they call a *mochado gorgio* a filthy gentile, or non-Gypsy; or by the even more contemptuous word *busno*.[2] The Gypsies like to keep their own language, Romani, a secret means of communicating among themselves, for this gives them an advantage when dealing with the police. The Romany words of warning, for instance, *plasta lesti* (which we might

1 Non-Gypsy gentiles.
2 "Barbarous foreigner."

ii

translate as "nix and scram"), when uttered by a Gypsy urchin for the benefit of his father, who is doing some illicit thimble-rigging in a fair, is enough to warn him that there is an interfering cop in the offing.

George Borrow, the Romany Rye,[3] possessed a knowledge of Romani that so enraged an old Gypsy witch, Mrs. Herne, that she tried to poison him with a cake she baked for him in her camp on the moors.[4] As the old Gypsy said to Borrow's successor, Leland, also a Romany Rye: "When people often ask what on earth good is the Romany tongue? I answers: 'Ye are all fools! There is plenty, plenty good in it, and plenty, plenty of our people would have been transported or hung but for the old, poor Roman language."

The Violin's Devilish Origin

With regard to the Gypsies' second possession, their special scale in music, there is no doubt that it is oriental, and so are its minute intervals, its conflicting rhythms, and its wealth of ornamental arabesques of sound. Incantation is the prototype of musical art, and music and poetry spring from oral magic as the horns of the lyre spring from the base of the instrument. In the East of Europe Gypsies have dances to bring rain, and they consider the scale in their music divine, and the violin, the instrument on which they play, supernatural. They ascribe its invention not to God but to the *Beng* or Devil, who by his magic helps the performer.

When in 1919 I consorted with my Gypsy blood-brother—an Austro-Hungarian prisoner, formerly a Gypsy *primas*[5] he told me the gypsy version of how the violin originated in far off Transylvania. It tells of Mara, a village girl whom the peasants thought bewitched, because no man asked her in marriage, in spite of her great beauty and rich dowry. She was in love with a farmer, but he would never cast a look her way, though she sighed for him from morn till eve. At last, finding all her efforts fruitless, she prayed to the Devil, and he said he would give her a magic instrument which would bring the young man to her feet. "But first of all," he said to her, "you must give me your father, your mother and your four brothers." The girl was bewitched, and she gave them all up without a murmur. Then, out of the body of the father the Devil made an instrument, and out of the white hair of the mother he fashioned a bow, and out of the four brothers he made the strings and strung them across the fiddle. "Now off with you," he said to the girl, "and play that fiddle of yours to the face of yonder youth, and he'll follow you to the ends of the earth." When the girl played, the young man followed her with his eyes set on her as if in a trance. And she took

3 A Romany Rye is a non-Gypsy who loves the race and has mastered the tongue, Romani.

4 Mrs. Herne was the mother-in-law of Borrow's Gypsy friend, Jasper Petulengro.

5 The leader of a group of Gypsy musicians.

his arm, and off they went, both of them full of joy. But suddenly the Devil appeared in their path and said: "Now it is time for me to collect my dues: both of you have listened to the Devil's instrument, and you must both come off with me to Hell." And off they went.

As for the violin, it lay on the ground in the forest until a rugged Gypsy happened to pass that way, and find it. And he is playing it yet throughout the world; and because it is the Devil's instrument men and women go daft when they hear its tones, and the Gypsy *primas* alone knows its secret.

When the Gypsies of the Great Band invaded Western Europe in 1417 from "Little Egypt" (the name they gave to the South of Greece) they inherited the tradition of the minstrel (*jongleur* or *juglar*) and their own incantations helped their magic, for music was associated with their shamanism or wizardry. They transformed the melodies they picked up, whether from the peasants or villagers, or from the more sophisticated people of the cities, for they were able to "cast the glamor" over them, as they said. And when they "played to the face" of their listeners they could even produce the effect of hypnotism. Hence the significance of the word "rhapsody," which means, according to its Greek origin, a sewing together of songs, for the minstrel must unite words and music so that the emotional excitement of his audience grows in intensity as the music progresses. Rhapsodies in Hungary always start with slow, sad music, the *lassu* meandering on in endless melancholy, for the Magyar enjoys himself weeping, according to the ancient Hungarian proverb, *sirva vigad a Magyar,* hence the slow, sad *lassu* that begins the rhapsody, leads on to the *lassu csardas,* with its building up of snap-rhythms before launching into the frenzied *friss csardas,* when all the people rise and take part in the vertiginous dance of the *csarda* or tavern, the national dance of the Magyar race. In Hungary and Transylvania, when following the Gypsy *patrin* or trail, I have collected magic dances in the villages from Gypsies whose skills as players of magic melodies and rhythms vie with those of witches and shamans when they play to your face.

The Tune of the Winter Solstice

On one occasion in 1925, when I was in Montenegro's capital, Cettinje, I came across a band of Gypsies from Zagreb with which I established contact, and they taught me a number of *Kolos* and *csardas* in return for a few rounds of Montenegrin rakija. Full of spirits and benevolence, they said they would play a special *bachtalo,* or lucky tune, and they started off with a tune which I immediately recognized as the main theme of the Pastoral Symphony by Beethoven.

iv

"Why that's Beethoven you're playing," I cried to the leader—a scraggy, dwarfish Gypsy with such a cast in his eye that I felt inclined to cross myself, lest he cast the evil eye upon me.

"Who's Beethoven?" said he, squinting. "I've never heard of him, but that is one of our old Croatian tunes—a song or dance that we always play 'round Christmastime when we go from house to house begging money and working spells."

"Who taught you that tune?"

"I've always known it; why shouldn't I? We Romanichals came into the world with tunes in our head. My father put a fiddle in my hands when I was three years of age."

"Ag," said another pock-marked Gypsy who was strumming a *gusla*,[6] "and our mothers sang to us when they gave us suck."

Although I noted down the tune as played rhapsodically by the Gypsies I still believed it was created by Beethoven, until some years later when I happened to play it for a friend. He enlightened me, saying that it was a traditional South Slav tune sung to strange, incomprehensible words, which referred to the ancient pagan ritual performed at the time of the Winter Solstice.

Gypsies have always been the humble priests of the practical religion of all country folk and peasants. With their magical ceremonies and quack cures they have been the *colporteurs* of what in Italy is still called *La Vecchia Religione,* or the cult of Diana, the Moon Goddess and her gospel of witches.

The *Bitchapen* or Magic Gift

I shall now give some examples of charms to cure disorders, which I came across in my travels. Among the Hungarians I was impressed by a strange cure for fever which they called *bitchapen* or gift, practiced by the Gypsies in Hungary. On Easter Monday they make a wooden box called the *bitchapen,* which is fashioned like a cradle with two sticks on the bottom. In this box they lay special herbs and amulets which everyone in the family touches. Then the box is enveloped in strips of white and red wool, which are wound round and round, and after everyone has spat upon it, it is carried by the oldest of the family to the nearest running stream. By doing this the Gypsies believe that they have conjured all the fevers and diseases which would have befallen them, into the box, and so transferred them to an anonymous scape-goat. The red wool symbolizes blood sacrifice, and the white wool is the biblical symbol of purity. As Leland observes in his reference to this Gypsy ceremony, it bears a close resemblance to the Jewish scape-goat. But woe to the unfortunate traveler who finds the box in the stream and opens it,

6 A primitive Serbian stringed instrument for accompanying the singing of folk ballads.

for he will receive the sum total of all the fevers exorcised by the Gypsies!

In the *bitchapen* ritual the running stream in which the box is left is significant. A more common cure for fever among Gypsies is to go to a running stream and cast pieces of wood nine times backward into the running water, repeating a magic rhyme as follows:

Fever go away from me
I give it, water, unto thee
Unto me thou art not dear,
Therefore go away from here.

The little poem ends with an invocation to *Mashmurdalo,* a giant of the woods who lurks in lonely places, hoping to waylay beasts or men and devour them.

The Magic of Garlic

The herb that fascinated me more than any other was garlic, for it was associated with my early University days when I studied Greek and Latin. My father was a friend of the late Sir James Fraser, the author of *The Golden Bough,* and whenever I had the opportunity I waylaid him, for he used to give me fascinating details about certain plants and herbs mentioned in Homer and Ovid. One day he gave me a disquisition on garlic, telling me that the magic herb *moly,* which Homer gave as a protection to Odysseus against the spells of the witch Circe, might have been garlic. In later years I used to meet the old man occasionally when he used to visit the Athenaeum in London, and I would bring him news about the magic properties of garlic which I had picked up among Gypsies in Hungary, Greece, Italy, and Spain.

One of my early adventures with garlic was during my long bout of gypsying in Hungary, Transylvania, and Roumania, when I had the strange experience of sleeping in a vampire-haunted graveyard. I discovered that garlic is an antidote to vampires, for I met a victim of the sinister demon in that graveyard who rebuked me for not carrying sprigs of garlic with me whenever I had to visit a cemetery that might be haunted by the evil *nachtsehr.* [7]

On another occasion in Sparta, when I was buying asfodels from a flower-seller who had a beautiful golden-haired little girl sitting on her lap, I murmured ecstatically, "What a beautiful child!" With a cry of dismay the mother pulled the child away from me, muttering the word *skodo* (garlic) under her breath, as if to ward off the evil eye. I then realized that, as in ancient Greek days, it was still perilous to awaken the jealousy of the immortal gods by praising mortal beings. I was told that

7 The night-haunting vampire, called by the Roumanians *strigoi.*

in Greece, even today mothers put leaves of garlic under the pillows of their children as a protective charm when they are asleep. As garlic turns black after a certain time, it was probably this phenomenon that gave rise to the popular belief that the plant absorbs evil into itself, hence its efficacy as a cure. Homer, when speaking of the herb in Book X of the *Odyssey*, notes that it was black at the root, but the flower was like to milk. Another detail about garlic that I heard in Turkey was that sailors in the Black Sea carried garlic as a protection against shipwreck.

Under The Bridges

Another obsession of mine in my Gypsy-wandering days in the past was Bridge-Lore, for among the weird race of Gypsies, the bridge has special significance. Many a time during my wanderings I have slept beneath bridges, whether in Hungary, Roumania, Greece or Spain, and I shall now tell a story which sprang from the very ancient traditions of the nomadic tribes. Let us not forget that the head of the ancient Roman religion was the Pontifex Maximus—the Chief Bridge-Maker, the priest who created the bridge between this life on earth and Heaven.

Among the Gypsies the "Song of the Bridge" is an expression of the belief in the necessity and efficacy of "Foundation Sacrifice," in order to secure the stability of Churches and bridges, especially the latter, in the primitive times when armies had to cross immense rivers such as the Danube, the Rhine, or the Ebro. The Song of the Bridge I heard for the first time in the East of Europe, but later it was sung and mimed for me among the tribes of nomad coppersmiths in different parts of the Western world. The song is based upon the belief that a living person has to be walled up in the bridge if it is to stand steadfastly through the ages. The song was sung for me by an old Gypsy woman, a Roumanian Gypsy called Pararchiva, a bronzed, wizened old hag, who was brimful of magical practices. No sooner did she begin the chant than she rolled her eyes and swayed her body to and fro. She told me the story first in rapid tones, as the rhythm worked its spell upon her, and as her Gypsy grandchildren beat their palms together to excite her:

"Manoli was a Gypsy mason, and with his two brothers he was building a bridge over the Danube. He dreamt that he would never be able to finish the bridge unless he sacrificed the first woman he met. Poor wretch—unlucky is the man who has dreamt, especially if they're nightmares, for nightmares are the devil's warning.

"At the hottest hour of the following day, when the Gypsies were taking their ease, lo and behold, Manoli saw his wife in the distance with the wives of his two brothers, and they were bringing the food.

Remembering his dream, Manoli said to himself, 'God protect me! Let not my wife be the first to reach the bridge.' But that day the devil had his way. Aye, it wasn't the wives of Manoli's two brothers who came up to the bridge, for they left the food on a stone and went their way. But the luckless Manoli saw his wife, the fair Lenka, coming towards him bringing his food.

'Ho there, Manoli! Here's your food I'm bringing,' she said. 'What ails you, man, Why such sadness in your life? Why, bless me, you're crying!'

Manoli, groaning, then told her the prophecy. 'Behold, wife of mine,' said he, 'there's no other way out: I must wall you up in the bridge if it is to span the river.'

'Give over foolishness,' said Lenka.

At this point the story became dramatic, as the witch described detail by detail the walling process and the dialogue that took place between Manoli and his wife as he built the wall about her.

When the bricks reached her neck she cursed him. "As soon as he finished his work," cried Parachiva, "he fell down into the water and sank to the bottom of the river, but his eyes stared up at the sky, and they became the eyes of the bridge."

When I was in Roumania I heard variants on the ritual of the Bridge or church foundation. Instead of walling up a living human being in the bridge, the Gypsy masons today measure the shadow of a stranger, a random passerby, with a piece of string which they afterward bury in the supports of the bridge or in the foundations of the church. But the shadow must be measured without the stranger being aware of it, for if he notices what has been done, his ghost will haunt the bridge or church for all eternity.[8]

As the actual president of the Gyspy Lore Society, Liverpool, I now wish to evoke the ghost of Charles Godfrey Leland, Founder and first President of our society; to summon him from his bank of asphodels in Shadowy Elysium and request him to tell us his version of the strangest and most fascinating word in all the Romany language—the word *zingan* or *tchenkan*, which is used in twenty or thirty forms by the peoples of every country except England to indicate the Gypsy. The word is connected with an ancient legend which states that when the Gypsies were driven out of India and arrived in Persia they constructed a wonderful machine to which a wheel was attached. But, alas, the Gypsies were unable to make the wheel revolve, and for this reason they could not travel further until the wheel would revolve. Nobody was able to turn it until one day an evil spirit presented himself under the disguise of

8 Jose Porta (with the collaboration of Walter Starkie), *Bajo los Puentes* (Barcelona, 1946).

a sage, and informed the chief, whose name was Chen, that the wheel would only turn when he had married his sister Guin. The chief accepted this advice, the wheel turned round, and the name of the tribe, after this incident, became that of the combined name of the brother and sister: Chenguin, the name of all the Gypsies in Turkey today. The legend states that in consequence of this incestuous marriage, the Gypsies were cursed and condemned by a Mohammedan saint to wander forever on the face of the earth.[9]

The real meaning of the myth, as Leland says, is very apparent. *Chen* is a Romany word, generally pronounced "chone", meaning the moon, while *guin* is almost universally given as *gan* or *kan*. *Chen-gan*, *chen-kan* or *zin-kan* are common Gypsy words for the sun. Thus *chen-kan* means "moon-sun." In Roumania I often heard the legend describing how the sun was a young man who fell in love with his own sister, and was condemned to wander forever in pursuit of her, after she was turned into the moon. This is, in fact, a spontaneous myth common to all races, and we have heard of it in Ireland, Borneo and Greenland. It was natural that the nomadic Gypsies, who observed that the sun and moon were forever wandering, should have identified their own nomadic life with the lives of these luminaries.

The beautiful ballad of the sun and the moon which exists in Roumanian as well as in Romani ends with the reckless declaration of the Sun that he chooses hell if he may have for a wife Helen of the shining silver hair. And so he descends from high heaven to see his sister Helen, and he puts on her body a transparent robe all embroidered in pearls. But woe to him and woe to her! During the service in the church the lights are all extinguished, the church bells crack while ringing, and the seats turn upside down. The bride is convulsed with fear, for suddenly an invisible hand seizes her, and having borne her on high, then casts her into the sea where she at once changes into a beautiful little silver fish. As for the sun, he grows pale and rises into the heavens, and descending in the West, he plunges into the sea to search for his sister Helen of the shining hair. However the Lord God takes the fish in his hand, casts it forth into the sky, and changes it into the moon.

Then He speaks. And while God is speaking the entire universe trembles, the peaks of the mountains bow down and shiver with fear.

"Thou Helen of the long silver tresses, and thou resplendent Sun, who art both free from all strain, I condemn you for eternity to follow each other with your eyes through space, without ever being able to meet or to reach each other upon the road of heaven. Pursue one another for all time in traveling around the skies and lighting up the world."

9 C. G. Leland, *The Gypsies* (New York, 1924), pp. 339-344.

"The Story of All Stories"
Envoy by the Romany Rye, C. G. Leland

Fallen from a high estate to sin, wicked, and therefore wandering: it was with such a story of being penitent pilgrims, doomed for a certain space to walk the earth, that the Gypsies entered Europe from India into Islam and into Christendom, each time modifying the story to suit the religion of the country which they invaded. Now I think that this sun and moon light is far from being frivolous, and that it conforms wonderfully well with the famous story which they told to the Emperor Segismund and to the Pope and all Europe that they were destined to wander because they had sinned. When they first entered Europe the Gypsies were full of these legends, they told them to everybody, but they had previously told them to themselves in the form of the Indian sun and moon story. This was the root from whence the stories grew. As the tale of the Wandering Jew typifies the Hebrew, so does this tale of the sun and moon typify the Romany.[10]

Introducing Jasper Petulengro

Here the Gypsy Gemman see
With his Roman jib and his rome and dree—
Ram and dree, ram and dry,
Rally round the Romany Rye.

It was thus that Jasper Petulengro, alias Ambrose Smith, and his Gypsy companions saluted their Romany Rye, George Borrow, when they bade him carouse with them outside the tents beside the caste of Ali on Mousehold Heath or elsewhere, whenever the Gypsy families of the Petulengros—the Boswells, Hernes, Youngs, Grays, Lees, Lovells, Maces, and Coopers—gathered at the horse-fairs or the prize-fights. Jasper had been more than a friend to Borrow even since youth, for they had done the Gypsy blood-ceremony together, a fact that was never forgotten by the Petulengro or blacksmith who was to become through the genius of the Romany Rye a world-famous character in literature. Jasper, in fact, was the Gypsy conscience of Borrow which at times pricked him and produced in him moments of remorse and dissatisfaction with the compromises he made with the "gentility" of gorgio society. The climax of Jasper's appeal to George's conscience comes in *Lavengro* in the great

10 C. G. Leland, *Ibid.,* pp. 345-347.

passage describing his meeting with his Gypsy brother, whom he had not seen in years.

"What is your opinion of death, Mr. Petulengro?" said I, as I sat down beside him.

"My opinion of death, brother, is much the same as that in the old song of Pharaoh which I have heard my grandson sing: When a man dies he is cast into the earth and his wife and child sorrow over him. If he has neither wife nor child, then his father and mother, I suppose; and if he is quite alone in the world, why, then he is cast into the earth, and there is an end of the matter."

"And do you think that is the destiny of man?"

"There's an end of him, brother, more's the pity."

"Why do you say so?"

"Life is sweet, brother."

"Do you think so?"

"I think so! There's the night and day, brother, both sweet things; sun, moon, and stars, brother, all sweet things; there's likewise a wind on the heath. Life is very sweet, brother; who would wish to die?"

"I would wish to die—"

"You talk like a gorgio—which is the same as talking like a fool. Were you a Romanichal you would talk wiser. Wish to die indeed! A Romanichal would wish to live forever!"

"In sickness, Jasper?"

"There's the sun and stars, brother."

"In blindness, Jasper?"

"There's the wind on the heath, brother; if I could only feel that, I would gladly live forever. Dorta, we'll go now to the tents and put on the gloves; and I'll try to make you feel what a sweet thing it is to be alive, brother!"[11]

Gypsy Petulengro, the author of *Romany Remedies and Recipes,* who claimed to be a descendant of Borrow's Gypsy hero, was a well known figure in England whose roving temperament carried him all over the world. Born in a caravan, his childhood was spent rambling over the English countryside learning, as he said, the two gypsy accomplishments: how to play the violin and how to use his fists. All his life he was an impenitent nomad, and his thirst for adventure carried him into wild places, from the jungles of the Amazon to the Australian bush country, and the gold fields of South Africa. In his early days he lived in Gypsy style, sometimes as a street musician in the cities, and at other times following the example of Jasper Petulengro's call to "the wind on the

---

11 George Borrow, *Lavengro* (London, 1951), pp. 159-160.

heath." In 1936 he published his autobiography, entitled *Gypsy Fiddler* by "Petulengro," edited by W.B. O'Hanlon, which gives a racy account of his adventures. Sometimes his love of snakes, which he must have inherited from Jasper, who was a *sapergro* or snake-fancier, landed him in difficulties. One day he was sitting outside his van engaged in feeding a ring-snake by forcibly stuffing small frogs down its throat. Hearing a noise between a cough and a snort, and looking up, he was confronted by a fair vision in a great poke-bonnet around which was a red band with a design of yellow flowers as a badge. At the moment, however, this vision's strong, handsome features were contorted into an expression of fury.

"How can you do such a wicked thing?" she demanded. "Have you no idea, boy, that it's a sin to inflict cruelty on God's creatures?"

Such was his introduction to Evangeline Booth, later Generalissimo of the Salvation Army. What she did not know was that snakes almost invariably refuse food when first in captivity, and will die unless one makes them eat.

Another adventure in the Petulengro tradition occurred when he was working as a horse-doctor at a fair in Kent. He was arrested by a policeman for "bishoping" a horse's teeth. This is a Gypsy's trick which consists of sculpturing an aged horse's teeth into the shape of a colt's by means of a red-hot iron. Petulengro had the misfortune to be brought up before a magistrate who rode with the local pack of hounds and was a great lover of horses. Unfortunately, he had heard of bishoping, which he called horse-torturing, and Petulengro was given a savage fine.[1][2]

Gypsy Petulengro's *Romany Remedies and Recipes* deserves to be widely read in these days when so many are becoming aware of the barren artificiality of our contemporary civilization and long to return to a saner and simpler pattern of life. As the author of this *vade mecum* of Romany remedies says, most of the complaints, with which the inhabitants of different countries are afflicted can be cured with the herbs that grow in those countries. Most of the medicines sold today were originally given in the form of Romany remedies. But astute manufacturers, having found out their real value, have given them new names, written and published frightening advertisements, and so induced people to spend much money on things which they could obtain for nothing, and which are more beneficial when taken in their natural form.

I rejoice to see included in the list of ointments the celebrated Romany balm which the Roumanian Gypsies used to tell me was their secret cure. They called it "Frog of the Horse Hoof."

12 Gypsy Petulengro, *Gypsy Fiddler* (New York, 1936).

PREFACE

My grandfather was the old gipsy tinker Petulengro immortalized by George Borrow in *The Romany Rye* and *Lavengro*. My father, who was his seventh son, was a 'grye-koper' (horse-dealer) and traded Welsh and Exmoor ponies with the Hungarian and Rumanian Zingari. It was while in Rumania that he met my mother, who came from the stock of Rumanian Zingari, and it was from my mother that I acquired my knowledge of herbs and remedies, which had been handed down by her ancestors for centuries. Many Romanys have forgotten the formulas, or have neglected their uses, but I have always held on to them, possibly because I had the good fortune to be taught to read and write, while most of my relations and friends are still unable to do so. I would like to record that what little education I had was mostly due to a well-known British admiral, Admiral Sir A. K. Wilson, V.C., and to his sister, who took a great interest in me when my parents were travelling in the district in which he lived when ashore. In return for teaching him Romany words he paid an old country lady to teach me, and I received my first lessons in her humble little cottage.

You must excuse me if my grammar is not all that it should be. I have done my best to make the remedies clear, and as most of them are simple to make, and the ingredients easy to procure, I hope there will be no difficulty in making up any of the recipes. There are many useful herbs and leaves which are often grown, and always can be grown, in one's own garden, though many folks are not aware of their value. I mention them here to draw attention to them.

Leaves of the following should be dried and stored: Ash, Blackberry, Black Currant, Camomile, Dandelion, Ground Ivy, Golden Rod, Horehound, Iceland Moss, Lobelia, Nettles, Peppermint, Plantain, Raspberry, Scabious, Rosemary, Southernwood, Sorrel, Thyme, *Violet, Sage, Wormwood, Yarrow.

Flowers of the following should also be stored: Camomile, Elder (*Sambucus nigra*), Red Clover, Hop, Marigold, and Safflower.

Also *Roots* of the Dandelion, Lily of the Valley, Male Fern, Marshmallow, Red Dock, Rhubarb, Solomon's Seal.

And *Barks* of the Alder (*Prinos verticillatus*), Ash, Oak, Birch, Cherry, Poplar, Willow (*Salix alba*).

All the above leaves, flowers, roots, and barks should be dried and packed in either envelopes or jars, and named, ready for any emergency. This, besides being very profitable, will be found to be a very interesting pursuit.

Most of the complaints which inhabitants of certain countries are afflicted with can be cured with the herbs that grow in that country. Nearly all the herbs mentioned in this book can be collected in your own lanes, and a lot of them grow in your own gardens (as many gardeners know too well), and they all are far more valuable than most of the things one takes a lot of trouble to grow. For instance, onions or cabbages can usually be purchased in the region of 1½*d.* per lb., but the common nettle, dried, would cost about 3*d.* per oz., or 4*s.* per lb., at the herbalist's.

Most of the medicines sold to-day at big prices under proprietary names were originally given to people in the form of Romany remedies. But astute manufacturers, having found out their real value, have commercialized them, given them new names, written and published frightening advertisements, and so induced folk to spend much money on things which they could obtain for nothing, and which are more beneficial when taken in their natural form. I have given, for example, one remedy for *blood-pressure*—the common stinging nettle—which (with spinach) contains all the necessary chlorophyll for softening hardened arteries. All the patent remedies for this ailment contain chlorophyll, but chlorophyll called by any other name is still chlorophyll.

There is one remedy in the book to which I would draw your especial attention, the *Romany Balm*, a recipe that is as old as the hills and scarcely ever fails to effect a cure of skin-complaints. A lady who had suffered for nineteen years with a terrible skin-complaint, and whose case had been given up as hopeless by her doctors, successfully treated herself with this ointment, and her friends called it a miracle.

Most of the herbs and ingredients which are printed in this book can be obtained from any herbalist (or chemist), but if in any doubt write to Gypsy Petulengro's Romany Remedy Co., 5 Heathcote Road, Boscombe, Hants., who will gladly supply you with any of them in packets. It is advisable when making up the medicines to make only enough for a week's supply. Usually the herbs to make one pint of medicine are in the packets mentioned above and a pint is generally 14 to 16 wineglassfuls, sufficient for a week's treatment.

I have marked with an asterisk the Violet leaf on page vi. This is the reason. An old Romany with whom I was acquainted treated a lady suffering from cancer. The lady lived for years after that and even advertised in the newspapers for my friend to thank her. I do not profess to cure cancer, but in this case it certainly saved this lady's life, according to her own story.

During the past thirty-five years I have devoted much of my time to lecturing on 'Old Romany Remedies and Recipes', and as a result I have had thousands of testimonials and letters of appreciation from people in the many countries in which I have travelled. On March 17, 1934, I was invited by the B.B.C. to broadcast about the origin of the British Romanys, and during the broadcast I mentioned the fact that the gipsies seldom visited the 'Mullah-Moosh-Engro', as we call the doctor, and told of a few simple remedies. As a result the B.B.C. had hundreds of letters asking that I should give a further broadcast, which I did on March 30, two weeks later, in the series 'In Town To-night'. On June 5, 1934, I was again invited to broadcast, this time about 'The Gipsies and Derby Day', and later I had the honour of being singled out from dozens who had broadcast to appear in every performance at Radiolympia from August 16 to 25, 1934. A little before then an article had appeared in the *Sunday Express* under the title of 'Talks on the Telephone', and as a result I had had over 2,000 letters, all asking for further gipsy remedies. I also write for that live little Lancashire journal, the *Bolton Evening News*, the editor having asked me to give his readers more remedies to fulfil the demand created by the success of those I had broadcast.

I hope this little book, which is designed to give the Romany remedies a rather more permanent form, will answer its purpose and be the means of giving relief or cure to many sufferers, and that the recipes (those which are not herbal), the Romany Poaching and Fishing Tricks, and the couple of little experiments to please the children, will cause you to place the volume in your bookcase to be ready at hand whether you want to catch eels or cure a complaint.

GIPSY PETULENGRO

November 1934

GERANIUM.

ARGEMONE.

MAGNOLIA.

CONTENTS

ALDER, EUROPEAN
(Alnus Glutinosa—Oak Family)

I
REMEDIES

NOTE.—*Most of the doses prescribed are given in measures of a wineglass. The glass referred to is the standard wineglass with a capacity of one-sixteenth of a pint.*

APERIENT

The bark of the Alder Tree (Prinos verticillatus).

Boil one ounce in a pint of water for five minutes.

Dose: A wineglassful at night.

N.B.—This is very like cascara and is one of the oldest Romany remedies.

APPENDICITIS

See 'Inflammation of the Bowels'.

ASTHMA AND CHEST COMPLAINTS

The leaves of the Sweet Chestnut Tree (Castana vesca).

Boil one ounce of the leaves to each one and a half pints of water for ten minutes. Strain and when cool add half ounce of honey and half ounce of glycerine.

Dose: A small wineglass upon rising and again after last meal.

N.B.—This is a recipe which has recently brought me in hundreds of testimonials of cures.

BURDOCK
(Arctium Lappa.)

BAD BLOOD, SCURVY, ERUPTIONS

Burdock Root (Arctium lappa).

Boil one ounce in one pint of water for five minutes.

Dose: A tablespoonful twice daily. In severe cases the dose can be taken more frequently.

BAD LEGS, ULCERS, ETC.

Lily (white pond) Root (Nymphoea odorata).

Boil two ounces of the root to one pint of water for twenty minutes. Gently apply the lotion when cooled to the legs, sores, or ulcers with a small piece of cotton wool, which should be used once only and burned. This is also a good lotion for many other kinds of sores and blotches.

N.B.—Use the Romany Balm after the above treatment.

BLADDER TROUBLES

Parsley Piert (Alchemilla arvensis).

Boil one ounce for a minute in one pint of water. Cool and strain.

Dose: A wineglassful twice a day.

See also 'Cystitis', 'Catarrh of the Bladder', 'Gravel' and 'Stone'.

BLOOD-PRESSURE

The common Stinging Nettle (Urtica dioica).

LILY ROOT
(White Pond Lily, Castalia Odorata,

Boil one ounce in one pint of water for five minutes. Strain and re-boil the liquid before bottling.

Dose: Take a small wineglassful three times daily.

N.B.—This is far better than the chlorophyll tablet products sold under fancy names at fancy prices.

BOILS AND CARBUNCLES (*both internal and external*).

Echinacea Root (Echinacea augustifolia).

Boil one ounce to each pint of water.

Dose: Take a wineglassful twice daily, and also dab a little of the solution on the affected parts when external.

See also 'Ointment for Boils'.

CATARRH

Procure some leaves of the horse-chestnut tree and dry them thoroughly. Then steep them in a solution of one ounce of saltpetre to quarter pint of warm water. Dry them again, then rub into a powder and burn on a tin plate and inhale the fumes at night. In the morning sniff up the nose a little of solution of common rock salt, one ounce to one pint of water.

CATARRH OF THE BLADDER

The herb Rupturewort (Herniaria glabra).

Boil one ounce in one pint of water for three minutes. Strain.

Dose: Take a wineglassful two or three times daily.

2

RASPBERRY

LOBELIA (TYPE OF HARDY VARIETIES).

LOBELIA (DWARF).

JALAP
(Ipomoea Jalapa)

CHILBLAINS

Use two pints of the water in which parsnips have been boiled (no salt must have been added). Mix in the liquid one tablespoonful of powdered alum. Stir well and bathe the hands (or feet) in the solution for twenty minutes. Then allow the solution to dry, without rinsing. Keep the solution for further use until the chilblains are quite gone.

COLDS

See 'Inhalent'.

CONSTIPATION

1 oz. Jalap Root, 1 piece of Aloes (the size of a pea), 1 pint of water.

Boil together for ten minutes. Strain and mash the root well so that you get all the moisture out.

Dose: A wineglassful morning and night.

CONSUMPTION

¼ oz. each of the herbs Mousear, Life Root, Liquorice Root, Golden Seal, Marshmallow Root, Iceland Moss; ½ oz. Linseed.

Boil together in one quart of water for twenty minutes. Add, afterwards, two tablespoonfuls of honey.

Dose: A wineglassful three times a day.

This is one of the finest remedies known, and in all but the most advanced cases will give relief. The

LICORICE ROOT
(Glycyrrhiza Glabra)

Romanys of all countries have given this recipe for many years, and I have had many letters telling me of the marked improvement after a week's treatment. Persons who are weak-chested, or have any affection of the lungs, or are troubled with a continual hacking cough, should get this remedy as soon as possible.

CORNS

See 'Gipsy Foot Ointment'.

COUGHS

¼ pint White Vinegar, 2 oz. Honey, ¼ oz. Black Liquorice, 1 Lemon.

Place the vinegar and the liquorice (broken up fine) in a basin. Put into a very hot oven and stir until liquorice dissolves. Add honey, and when cooling add the juice of the lemon. Instead of putting into the oven, the vinegar and liquorice can be boiled in an enamelled pan over a very gentle heat on the gas stove.

Dose: Take a teaspoonful whenever the cough is troublesome. It is an excellent thing for children with weak chests and is a preventive as well as a remedy.

CYSTITIS, NEPHRITIS, AND BLADDER COMPLAINTS

Couch Grass Root (Agropyrum repens).

Boil one ounce in one and a half pints of water for five minutes. Strain.

WINTERGREEN
(Gaultheria Procumbens)

Dose: A wineglassful five or six times a day if possible.

DEAFNESS

The fat of the 'Hotchi-witchi' (the hedgehog).

Melt the fat and pour a drop into the ear at night. This relieves the ear-drum and dissolves the hard wax which is the frequent cause of deafness. This is a fine old gipsy remedy. A good substitute for the hedgehog fat is the fat of the ordinary goose. Melt a little of this and drop a little of it, warm, in the ear when in bed, and sleep lying on the opposite ear. Next night do the other ear. Many obstinate cases of deafness have been overcome by this treatment. I cured myself thus when I had a bad attack of deafness some years ago. People who are what is often called 'a little hard of hearing' should try this remedy without delay. It will possibly save them from going in time completely deaf.

DIABETES

The herb Periwinkle (Vinca major).

Boil one ounce to one and a half pints of water for ten minutes.

Dose: A wineglassful three times daily.

This treatment is used by many South African doctors with good results.

DIARRHOEA

Rhubarb Root.

Boil one ounce for five minutes in one pint of water.

BROOM
(Cytisus Scoparius.)

Dose: A small dose will cure diarrhoea. A large one is a safe aperient.

See also 'Infantile Diarrhoea' and 'Relaxed Bowels'.

DROPSY

The herb Broom (Cytisus scoparius).

Boil one ounce to each pint of water for ten minutes.

Dose: A tablespoonful three times daily.

N.B.—This is also a good tonic for the kidneys.

DYSPEPSIA

Mandrake Root (Podophyllum peltatum).

Boil one ounce in one pint of water for five minutes.

Dose: A teaspoonful five or six times daily if possible.

N.B.—This is one of the finest herbs in the world and promotes a good complexion as well as curing many little complaints.

Another remedy:

Quassia Chips.

Boil one ounce in a quart of water for five or six minutes.

Dose: A tablespoonful of the strained liquor after each meal.

EPILEPSY

Valerian Root (Valeriana officinalis).

Boil one ounce of the root in one and a half pints of water till reduced to one pint.

NOTES AND RECIPES

OAK

Dose: A small wineglassful four or five times a day.
See also 'St. Vitus' Dance'.

EYE AFFLICTIONS
See 'Eye Ointment' and 'Inflamed Eyes'.

GASTRITIS
Oak Bark.

Boil one ounce of oak bark in one quart of water until the liquid is the colour of whisky.

Dose: A wineglassful after each meal. This is called *Decoctum Quercus.*

GOUT
1 oz. Woundwort (Stachis palustri), 1 oz. Powdered Rhubarb Root (Rheum palmatum), 1 oz. Willow Bark (Salix alba).

Boil together in three pints of water for fifteen minutes. Strain.

Dose: Take two tablespoonfuls night and morning.
N.B.—*See also* 'Sciatica'.

GRAVEL
The herb Clivers or Cleavers.

Boil one ounce to one and a half pints of water for ten

BLACK CURRANT
(Ribes Nigrum, Saxifrage Family)

minutes. Strain and boil the liquid up again for one minute.

Dose: A wineglassful twice daily, morning and night.

HAIR STIMULANT

Rosemary (Rosemarinus officinalis).

Boil one ounce in a pint of water for five minutes. Rub the liquid well into the scalp at night.

See also 'Baldness'.

HEADACHE

See 'Neuralgia'.

HEART, MUSCULAR WEAKNESS OF

Kola Nut (Cola vera).

Boil one ounce in one and a half pints of water for ten minutes. Strain the liquid and bottle in tightly corked bottles.

Dose: A small wineglassful twice daily, preferably before meals.

N.B.—This is an excellent tonic for the nerves also.

HOARSENESS

Black Currant leaves.

Boil one ounce in one pint of water. Strain and bottle.

Dose: A tablespoonful two or three times a day.

BARBERRY
(Berberis Vulgaris, Barberry Family)

INDIGESTION

See 'Dyspepsia'.

INFANTILE DIARRHOEA

Cranesbill Root (Geranium malculatum).

Boil one ounce of the root in one and a half pints of water for twenty minutes (or until the liquid is reduced to one pint).

Dose: A small wineglassful twice daily.

N.B.—This also serves to stop bleeding internally, and is a good kidney tonic.

INFLAMED EYES, GRIT IN EYES, ETC.

One pennyworth of Bluestone.

Place enough to cover a sixpence in an ordinary eight-ounce medicine bottle. Fill with water that has been boiled. Shake until the bluestone has dissolved. Use with an ordinary eyebath.

N.B.—This will make the eyes smart slightly but will clear away obstructions and clean the eyes from grit. Diluted still further, it makes an excellent eyewash and eye strengthener for everyday use.

INFLAMMATION OF THE BOWELS (*now called Appendicitis*).

First of all take a tablespoonful of Lucca oil and place hot salt bags over the affected part. The bags

NOTES AND RECIPES

BLUE COHOSH

can be made of old pieces of calico filled with ordinary rock salt and heated in the oven. While one bag is being used others will be getting hot. Change the bags frequently. Make up meanwhile a liquor of elder flower water (by infusing one ounce elder flowers in a pint of water, as you would make tea). Add to this quarter ounce oil of peppermint, stir well and give the patient frequent doses of a small wine-glassful.

This treatment has saved many lives and will usually avoid an operation.

INFLUENZA

See 'Inhalent'.

INHALENT

4 oz. of ordinary cheap grade Eau-de-Cologne, ¼ oz. of Formalin.

Shake well and keep in tightly stoppered bottle.

Rub a little between the palms of the hands and draw in deeply through the nostrils.

This, if persistently used, is a preventative of 'Flu' and the common cold. No germ can live near it. A drop or two can be sprinkled on the handkerchief or the pillow without damaging the fabrics.

INSOMNIA

The flowers of the Cowslip (Primula veris).

Infuse as you would if making tea. Let it stand for

RHUBARB

NOTES AND RECIPES

five minutes. Milk can be added and it can be drunk at bedtime.

A small pinch of Isinglass will make the infusion act as a remedy for Brain Fatigue.

See also 'Neuralgia' and 'Isinglass' (Appendix, page 46).

ITCH,   SCABIES,   AND   OTHER   PARASITIC
    COMPLAINTS

See under 'Ointments'.

JAUNDICE

The herb Barberry Bark (*Berberis vulgaris*).

Boil one ounce in one pint of water for twenty minutes. Squeeze out the bark and strain the liquor.

Dose: A tablespoonful three or four times a day.

KIDNEY COMPLAINTS

See 'Dropsy' and 'Infantile Diarrhoea'.

LIVER DISORDERS

See 'Rheumatism'.

LUMBAGO

Two pennyworth of Venice Turpentine (*not synthetic*).

This is a sticky substance like very thick treacle. Mix

YELLOW DOCK
(Rumex Crispus, Buckwheat Family)

with ordinary flour until it is the consistency of dough. Form this into pills the size of a small pea.

Dose: Take two or three pills before retiring. Drink a glass of cold water afterwards. It usually settles the worst case of lumbago in six or seven hours and the pills do not purge.

Therefore even if more than two or three are taken no discomfort follows.

N.B.—This is a genuine Romany recipe that scarcely ever fails.

LUNG TROUBLES

See 'Consumption' and 'Coughs'.

MENSTRUAL IRREGULARITIES

Blue Cohosh Root (Calilphyllum thalictroides).

Boil two ounces in three pints of water for twenty minutes. Strain the liquid and bottle.

Dose: A wineglassful twice a day.

MENSTRUATION (SUPPRESSED), STONE, ETC.

The herb Liferoot (Senecis aureus).

Boil one ounce of the herb in one pint of water for a couple of minutes and strain.

Dose: Take small doses of a tablespoonful four or five times a day.

GROUND IVY

NERVES

Potassic Tartrate of Iron.

Mix half ounce with a pint of boiling water and bottle.

Dose: Take a teaspoonful twice a day.

Although this is not a Herb it is one of the finest remedies for nerves. We shall be pleased to supply it from 5 Heathcote Road, Boscombe, Hants.

NEPHRITIS

See 'Cystitis'.

NEURALGIA, HEADACHES

The herb Ladies' Slipper Root (Cypripedium pubescene).

Boil one ounce in a pint of water for ten minutes. Strain and bottle liquor.

Dose: A wineglassful when the attacks are on, and as a sleep-inducer on retiring at night.

OBESITY

The herbs Bladderwrack, Cordova, Boldo, Rhubarb.

Mix together. They can be made into a 'tea', or, better still, into tablets. The tablets made to the Romany formula can be obtained from the firm mentioned in the Preface under the name of '*Obesity Tablets*'.

PLEURISY ROOT
(Asclepias Tuberosa, Milkweed
Family)

PILES (INTERNAL)

The Yellow Dock Root (Rumex crispus).

Boil one ounce in one and a half pints of water. Strain.

Dose: A wineglassful night and morning.

PILES (EXTERNAL)

Make an ointment as follows:

4 oz. Pure Lard (no salt must be in it), 1 oz. of the leaves of the Plantain, ½ doz. leaves of the Ground Ivy.

Place all together in an enamelled pan and boil together over gentle heat for about ten minutes. Press the leaves well in the lard to get out all the goodness; strain into a jar and use when cool. Put the ointment freely into the rectum at night.

N.B.—Both the treatments can be used at the same time.

PLEURISY

The herb Pleurisy Root (Asclepis tuberosa).

Boil one ounce in one and a half pints of water for ten minutes. Strain.

Dose: A wineglassful two or three times a day.

QUINSY

The herb Cudweed.

Boil one ounce in one pint of water for one minute.

SPEARMINT
(Mentha Viridis—Mint Family)

Dose: A tablespoonful twice daily.

N.B.—Can also be used as a throat gargle.

RELAXED BOWELS

The herb Agrimony.

Infuse as if making tea, one ounce of the herb in one pint of boiling water.

Dose: A tablespoonful two or three times a day.

See also 'Diarrhoea'.

RHEUMATISM

Dandelion Root.

Boil one ounce in one and a half pints of water for twenty minutes, making up to one pint after allowing for evaporation. Strain.

Dose: A wineglassful of the liquor twice daily.

This is called by the chemists *Decoctium Tarascaci.*

N.B.—It is also good for liver disorders.

SCIATICA

The herb Ragwort.

Infuse one ounce in one pint of water as if making tea. Strain off and bottle.

Dose: A wineglassful three times a day.

See also under 'Liniments', page 23.

SCURVY

See 'Bad Blood'.

MALE FERN

SICKNESS AND FLATULENCE

The herb Spearmint (Mentha viridis).

Boil one ounce in a pint of water for two minutes.

Dose: A tablespoonful three or four times a day or whenever the sickness is felt.

SORE THROATS

The herb Selfheal (Prunella vulgaris).

Make an infusion of the herb, as if making tea, using one pint of water to one ounce of the herb.

Dose: Drink very slowly a wineglassful twice or three times a day.

ST. VITUS' DANCE

Black Cohosh Root (Cimicefuga racemosa).

Make a liquor by boiling one ounce in one and a half pints of water. Continue boiling until reduced to one pint, then strain, and bottle balance of liquor.

Dose: Varies from a teaspoonful for a child to a wineglassful for an adult, and should be taken three times a day.

See also 'Epilepsy'.

STONE IN THE BLADDER AND OTHER URINARY COMPLAINTS

The herb Gravel Root (Eupatorium purpureum).

Boil one ounce in one and a half pints of water for twenty minutes. Strain and bottle the resultant liquor.

HOUSE LEEK
(Sempervivum Tectorum.)

Dose: A small wineglassful taken frequently—five or six times a day.

TAPEWORMS

Male Fern Root (Dryopteris filixmas).

Boil one ounce in one and a half pints of water till reduced to one pint.

Dose: Take no food for a few hours before retiring, and in the morning take a wineglassful of the liquor. In the case of children, give doses of a tablespoonful three times a day before food.

ULCERS

See 'Bad Legs'.

WHOOPING-COUGH

The herb Mousear (the common Hawkweed).

Boil one ounce in a pint of water for three minutes.

Dose: A wineglassful three or four times a day. Add a spoonful of brown sugar to each dose at the time of taking. This will work wonders. It is also a particularly good tonic for children.

GOLDEN SEAL
(Hydrastis Canadensis, Crowfoot Family.)

VINCA ROSEA.

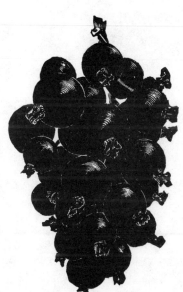

RIBES (BLACK CURRANT).

NETTLE
(Urtica Dioica, Nettle Family)

II

OINTMENTS, EMBROCATIONS, AND LINIMENTS

BALDNESS (ALOPECIA) OINTMENT

2 oz. Pure Hog Lard, 1 dr. of Chrysorobin.

Mix thoroughly and rub some well into the scalp. Be very careful that it does not get into the eyes as it causes severe smarting.

See also 'Hair Stimulant'.

BALM ('ROMANY BALM')

The secret of the Albanian and Rumanian Zingari.

4 oz. of the fat from the kidney of the pig, 1 oz. of cuttings from the 'Frog' of the horse hoof,* 1 Houseleek (the plant that grows on the tiles of cottages and outbuildings, a rosette-shaped plant), 1 oz. scrapings of the bark of the Elder tree.

Place altogether in an enamelled pan over a slow heat. Stir while the fat is 'sizzling', then strain off (after half an hour's simmering) into a clean jar and use on any sores, skin-complaints, cuts, boils, bruises, etc.

During the summer of 1934, a lady who had suffered with a terrible skin-complaint for nineteen years made her own ointment from this Romany recipe and cured herself with it, after many expensive treatments by doctors had failed.

---

* The horse-hoof clippings can be obtained from any farrier, who usually throws them away.

THYME
(Thymus Vulgaris)

BEAUTY OINTMENT

2½ oz. Spermaceti, ½ pint Almond Oil, 1 oz. White Wax, ¼ oz. Benzoin (coarse powder), ½ oz. Prepared Calamine.

Melt together in a gentle heat. Strain through a very fine sieve (rubbing it through if difficult to strain) and keep in airtight jars.

Use freely at night. In the daytime, use sparingly as a base for face-powder.

N.B.—This wonderful skin food is used by the beautiful 'Romany chis' all the world over.

BOIL AND EROSION OINTMENT

4 oz. Resin (in coarse powder), 2 oz. Yellow Wax, 8 oz. Lard, 1 oz. (Fluid) Almond Oil, ¼ oz. Boric Powder.

Melt together in gentle heat. Strain through a fine muslin or a piece of flannel and stir while it cools. Apply to boils. Where possible use a bandage of old linen (never use new material).

EUCALYPTUS OINTMENT

1 oz. Eucalyptus Oil, 2 oz. Hard Paraffin, 2 oz. Soft Paraffin.

Melt together and stir well while it is cooling.

EYE OINTMENT

For Inflamed Eyelids, Sore or Red Eyes.

¼ oz. Red Mercuric Oxide, 1 oz. Purified Coco-nut Oil, ¾ oz. Pure Lard.

QUASSIA
(Picraenia Excelsa)

Mix well together when warmed, and use on the eyelids when cool.

N.B.—This ointment has been used for years with success.

FACE OINTMENT (GIPSY BEAUTY CREAM)

1 oz. Red Dock Root, 2 oz. Cold Cream, 2 oz. Pure Pork Lard, 2 oz. Elder tree flowers.

Place the lard in an earthen jar, cut up the dock root, and add with the elder tree flowers to the lard. Heat for one hour. Strain, add the cold cream, and mix well together until cold.

This is a fine remedy for blackheads.

GIPSY FOOT OINTMENT

4 oz. Tallow, 1 oz. Powdered Sulphur, 1 oz. (Fluid) Olive Oil.

Melt together and stir well while it is cooling. Rub a little on the feet before a walk. No corns will ever appear if you use this.

N.B.—This ointment is used by the nomads of the Balkan States, whose main method of transport is walking.

HOUSEHOLD OINTMENT

1 oz. Boric Acid (the fine powder), 2 oz. Hard Paraffin, 4 oz. Soft Paraffin.

Melt together and stir well until cold.

JUNIPER
(Juniperus Communis, Pine Family)

ITCH, SCABIES, AND OTHER PARASITIC COMPLAINTS OINTMENT

2 oz. Mercury, 2 oz. Lard.

Mix well together until all the little metal globules are invisible and the lard turns dark. First wash the affected parts in hot water, then apply the ointment. This is best done at night before retiring. Where the hands are affected, especially between the fingers, they should be well smeared and an old pair of gloves worn whilst sleeping.

PILES OINTMENT

See 'Piles' (page 15).

SIMPLE OINTMENT

4 oz. Pure Lard, 1 oz. Boracic Powder.

Mix well together.

EMBROCATION FOR SPRAINS

½ pint White Vinegar, ½ pint Turpentine, ¼ pint Methylated Spirit, ½ oz. Opodeldso (from the chemist), the whites of two eggs.

Mix together in the above order, then bottle and stand aside for a couple of days, shaking the bottle occasionally. After two days the embrocation will be ready for use.

LINIMENT FOR GOITRE

1 part Sassafras, 9 parts Lucca Oil.

ANISE SEED

NOTES AND RECIPES

Rub well into the affected part. Sleep at night with a little on a piece of linen round the neck.

LINIMENT FOR SCIATICA, ETC.

1 dr. Wintergreen (extract), 4 oz. Olive Oil, 1 oz. Succinic Oil.

Mix together and shake well before using.

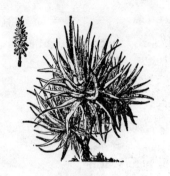

ALOE
(Aloe Vera—Lily Family)

VIOLET (SINGLE).

CERASTIUM.

ACHILLEA MILLEFOLIUM.

BIRD CHERRY
(Prunus Padus—Rose Family)

III
RECIPES

'CLEARING' BEERS

Mix up half an ounce of isinglass in a small quantity of beer, which should be slightly warmed. Pour some of this into the 'bung-hole' of the cask before hammering in the bung. A little placed in each bottle will make it as clear as crystal.

HERB BEER

2 oz. Burdock Leaves, 1 oz. Yarrow, 1 oz. Dandelion Herb, 8 oz. Malt, 1 oz. Hops, 2 oz. Sugar, 1 oz. Yeast.

Place all except the sugar and yeast in a large pan with ten pints of water. Boil for two hours (gently simmering after it has once boiled). Strain off the liquor into an earthenware pan if possible (if not, an enamelled pan). When the liquor is just 'blood warm' stir in the sugar and the yeast. Let it stand in a warm place for twenty-four hours. Place a piece of cloth over the pan during this time. After that time has elapsed, skim off the yeast that has risen to the top and bottle the liquor (in screw-top bottles for preference), putting the corks 'lightly' into the bottles at first. Twelve hours later tighten them up. Stand away for a day or two, and the brew will be ready to drink.

N.B.—It is advisable to mix the yeast and the sugar together before pouring into the bulk of the brew, using a little of the cooled liquor to mix them with.

HOARHOUND
(Marrubium Vulgare, Mint Family.)

HOREHOUND AND WORMWOOD TONIC BEER

1 oz. Horehound, 1 oz. Wormwood, 1 oz. Hops, 8 oz. Malt, 10 pints of water, 2 oz. Brown Sugar, 1 oz. Yeast.

Boil together (all except the sugar and yeast) for two hours, lowering to a simmer after the liquor has once been brought to the boil. Strain through muslin into a large earthenware vessel, if possible (use an enamelled pan otherwise). Add the yeast and sugar, which should have already been mixed with a drop of the liquid when it had reached blood heat. Stir well into the bulk of the liquor and finish off bottling exactly as you would the beers and stouts in other recipes.

If you wish to make a quantity you can use a barrel or small cask, which, if kept for a few weeks, will increase in strength. Leave the large bung out for a couple of days after filling the cask, then hammer it well in and leave for six months if possible. The result will astonish you whether you use the Beer or the Stout recipe.

TONIC STOUT

1 oz. Nettles, 1 oz. Hops, 8 oz. Black (or burnt) Malt, ¼ oz. Black Liquorice, 2 medium-sized Potatoes, 2 oz. Brown Sugar, 1 oz. Yeast.

First add the herbs, malt, and hops to ten pints of water. Boil up and add the liquorice and the potatoes. The latter should be washed well *but not peeled,* and should be perforated with a fork or darning needle. Gently simmer until you have about eight pints of the liquor left. Turn out into earthenware pan if possible, after straining, and then stir in the yeast and sugar,

LILY OF THE
VALLEY

which should have been mixed beforehand with a little
of the liquor cooled in a cup or jug. Stir well into the
liquor. Stand in a warm place for twenty-four hours
and bottle in exactly the same manner as described in
the Herb Beer recipe.

If you want the 'ruby' tint, add an apple and a few
rusty nails for the 'iron'.

Leave for a couple of days after corking and watch
the beautiful creamy stout when poured out.

N.B.—*Don't shake the bottle when uncorking.*

TO DESTROY FLIES AND OTHER INSECTS

Spray with a solution of one ounce of formaldehyde
mixed with a quart of water.

A little of this solution should be placed in a saucer
in the summer-time when flies are troublesome. They
drink, and immediately die.

TO DESTROY MOTHS, BEETLES, ETC.

Dust a powder called 'Bitter Apple' around their
haunts, and sprinkle a little amongst clothes. No moth
or larva can survive this.

TO DRESS SKINS OF RABBITS, ETC.

Stretch out the pelt, or, better still, nail it on to a
door or piece of board. Scrape off as much of the
'fatty inner skin' as you can, using an old blunt knife

SOLOMON'S SEAL
(Convallaria Multiflora)

for the purpose. Mix up the 'dressing solution' as follows:

8 oz. Alum in powder, 2 pints boiling water.

Rub this solution well over the inside of the skin and when dry repeat. Next boil a handful of oak bark in a quart of water for a few minutes and 'wash' over the skin with this and dry again. These operations will take a week if a successful job is to be made of the skin. Untack the skin and rub into it

2 oz. Olive Oil, 2 oz. Linseed Oil.

This will make the skin beautifully supple. Lay the skin on a sheet of brown paper, fur uppermost, and dust over with a mixture of

1 oz. Alum, 1 oz. Bitter Apple.

Leave this in the fur for a couple of days. Brush well and rub skin to make it nice and soft.

TO PREVENT COLDS ON THE CHEST

Rub ordinary tallow candle (wax candles are of no use) on a piece of coarse brown paper. Place the paper with greased side next to the skin under vest. No matter how piercing the wind it will never penetrate this. The above can also be used to keep the feet dry and warm. Cut the paper to the shape of the foot and place inside the sock or stocking. Incidentally it will prevent callouses on the bottom of the feet.

TO PREVENT MILK FROM TURNING SOUR IN HOT WEATHER

Add one or two drops only of formalin to each pint of milk. This will kill all the bacteria and germs.

BRAMBLE
(Rubus Villosus, Rose Family)

Meat will not become tainted if washed in water to which a few drops of formalin has been added.

This is also a wonderful tip to persons suffering from body odour. Dab a little under the armpits with a sponge.

WOUND WORT
(Prunella Vulgaris, Mint Family)

TAGETES (MARIGOLD), DWARF FRENCH, GOLD STRIPED.

SCABIOSA (DWARF DOUBLE).

SCABIOSA (TALL).

PEPPERMINT
(Mentha Piperita)

IV

FOR THE KIDDIES

TRANSFERS

Prints can be taken from any newspapers or 'comics' direct to the scrap-book, in the following manner:

Rub the page of the book to which you wish to transfer the print with a piece of ordinary wax candle. Lay the print to be reproduced face downwards on to the waxed portion. Then rub over the back of the print with the handle of a metal spoon, using pressure, for a minute or so. Withdraw the print and the transfer will be left behind.

This will amuse the children for hours on a wet day.

FIRE PICTURES

Get some sheets of tissue paper about nine inches long by four inches wide. Turn down the edges about half an inch all round so as to form a stand. Mark over the paper any design, or name, with a solution of saltpetre (one ounce mixed with two ounces of water). Make sure that the design or name is continuous, with no breaks in the lines. Make a star with ink or pencil at the starting-point of the drawing. Then thoroughly dry the paper. Upon touching it now with a red-hot hat-pin or piece of wire at the point where the star is marked, the paper will slowly smoulder away where the solution has touched it, i.e., where the

MILFOIL
(Achillea Millefolium, Aster Family)

name or design has been drawn. Great astonishment
will be caused, especially if you have marked the names
of the children without their knowing it, and then tell
them the 'Fire Fairy' will write their names on request.
Try this at the children's parties. It causes endless fun.

SAFFRON
(Carthamus Tinctorus.)

V
DOG HINTS

DISTEMPER IN DOGS

In bad cases give the dog ordinary brewer's yeast, a small dose every morning.

TO PREVENT DISTEMPER

Give the dog a small piece of raw potato occasionally.

FOR MANGE

Make up an ointment of the following ingredients:

2 dr. Powdered Boracic Acid, 60 gr. Thymol, 2 oz. Soft Paraffin.

Rub this well into the skin every day. This remedy soon effects a cure.

A GOOD PILL FOR A DOG

Roll up a small piece of tobacco (the hard tobacco is best) in a piece of dough. If a dog has this frequently it will keep him in good condition and generally prevent worms.

FOR A DOG THAT HAS TAKEN POISON

First of all give him about 15 grains of emetic tartar.

FRAGRANT VALERIAN
(Valeriana Officinalis, Valerian Family)

This will make him vomit. After vomiting is finished, give him 2 oz. of castor oil.

This remedy scarcely ever fails to put him right.

SORE FEET IN DOGS

Some dogs, especially those that run about a lot, get a complaint which makes their 'nails' crack underneath. First wash their feet in a brine of common rock salt: one ounce to a quart of warm water. Then paint the sore parts with arnica.

TO CURE DOGS OF TICKS, FLEAS, ETC.

Make up the following solution:

2 oz. of crushed Stavesacre Seeds, 2 oz. of Quassia Chips, 2 oz. of Acetic Acid, 2½ pints of water.

Directions: First boil the quassia chips in the water for a minute or two, then add the stavesacre seeds and acetic acid while the solution is cooling. When cool, strain and sponge over the dogs every day for a week. When the fleas, etc., are all gone sponging need only be done about every fourteen days as a preventative.

WORMS IN DOGS

Don't feed the dog after midday, and the next morning give him grated areca nut with a piece of butter. When he wants to drink give him water in which carrots have been boiled. This is a good preventative also. Don't feed the dog for four hours after he has had the grated areca nut.

LABRADOR TEA
(Ledum Latifolium, Heath Family)

TO MAKE YOUR DOG'S COAT SHINE LIKE SILK

Shake out of a pepper-box boracic acid powder, and rub well into the coat with the tips of the fingers. Leave the powder in for an hour and then brush out. This will also prevent the dog from scratching, and you will notice that he will get to like it, become more contented, and naturally, therefore, get sleek and fat.

TO MAKE A 'NEW' DOG FOLLOW YOU AND NEVER LEAVE YOU TO FOLLOW OTHERS

Place a piece of soft bread under the armpit until it is permeated with your perspiration. Then give it to the dog.

ICELAND MOSS

RUBUS (BLACKBERRY, EARLY HARVEST).

RUBUS (RASPBERRY, THE HANSELL).

GERMANDER
(Teucrium Canadensis, Mint Family)

VI
FISHING, POACHING, AND OTHER TRICKS AND RECIPES

FISH BAIT FOR CATCHING TROUT AND EELS

Equal parts of:

Oil of Rodium, Oil of Juniper, Oil of Cedarwood.

Sprinkle a little of the mixture over a handful of moss and place the worms in the moss for at least twelve hours.

If using other bait, mix a drop of the oils with it.

BAIT FOR ROACH AND PERCH

Take equal parts of:

Oil of Spike, Oil of Fennel, Oil of Thyme.

Mix well together before using. Just a drop to any living or other bait.

BOLTING RABBITS (OR RATS) FROM THEIR HOLES

Get some coarse brown paper and cut it into strips about eighteen inches long and two inches wide. Make up a solution of the following:

4 oz. Saltpetre, ½ oz. Cayenne Pepper, enough Vinegar to make a 'pasty' solution.

Brush over the paper with this solution and then roll the paper into loose rolls. Dry them well before using.

WITCH GRASS
(Agropyron Repens)

Now place one of the rolls of paper into the hole on the windward side, light it up, and lay a piece of turf over the hole when it is well alight. Watch the other hole or place a net over it. When shooting this way half a doxen holes can be worked at once. If netting them, place nets over bolt-holes before lighting up the paper rolls.

DRAWING RABBITS OR HARES TO YOUR FIELDS

Mix together the following:

¼ oz. *Oil of Parsley*, *1 dr. Oil of Angelica*, *1 dr. Oil of Aniseed*, ½ oz. *Oil of Copaiba*.

Place a few drops on pieces of wood or twigs and lay about the spots where you wish the animals to come.

TO KEEP RATS AND MICE AWAY FROM YOUR PREMISES

Soak pieces of calico in spirits of tar and place a piece near each hole.

PRIMROSE
(Primula Veris)

FAKES

During my travels I have seen, in market-places, exhibitions, and stores, practically every kind of fake worked, and I append here several of the old 'Evergreens'—that is, fakes that have been 'worked' till they have become stale, and then resurrected again.

I was once on a market and saw a 'grafter' selling a most wonderful preparation for keeping away flies from meat, fish, etc. Flies were humming around everywhere in millions, but this was his offer: 'Ten dollars if a fly alights on the meat or fish displayed on my stall.' Around the fish and meat were the 'Fly Preventives', which were being handed out like hot pies, at a dime apiece. Some flies, more daring than their mates, hovered around, but never went within a foot of the meat and fish, while the crowd waited around anxiously to try and get the ten dollars. No one, however, was lucky, and at the end of the day's 'pitch' the 'grafter' smilingly packed up his 'traps' and went away. Now, it wasn't the 'Fly Preventives', at a dime apiece, that kept the flies away, but the fact that the 'grafter' had soaked the fish and meat in paraffin. But of course the buyers of the 'Preventive' did not have the same 'smelling powers' as the flies and were easily caught.

There are many fakes that are always being sold, some good, some bad, some indifferent, but generally if the secret of them is known they can easily be made. I give some of them here, and I am sure some of my readers will find them useful, and, even if they only

WILD GINGER
(Asarum Canadense)

use them as tricks or experiments, many will be pleased just because they 'know how they're done'.

TOOTH POWDER

This is the recipe of the *Tooth Powder King*, whom I met during my travels in the United States of America:

1 oz. Powdered Cuttle Fish, 1 oz. Prepared Chalk, ¼ oz. Powdered Orris Root.

He confided to me that this was the 'Cooshti chat', which means the 'real goods'. I have used it myself. It costs very little to make and is the best I know.

CORNS AND BUNIONS

The remedy for Corns and Bunions of 'Percy' the 'corn faker', another American 'grafter', was 'collodion'. Percy had a knack of breaking away a big callous after dabbing on a little of this cure, and certainly collodion is a good corn and bunion remedy.

SHINEWHITE

A good old 'perennial' is a 'polishing powder' (or 'paste') usually called 'Shinewhite', but also by any other old name according to where it is being sold. This is how to make the best shinewhite, and the recipe is certainly good and cheap to make. Buy from the oil shop two balls of whiting. Break them up and dissolve in a pail of water, stirring around until the fluid is just like milk to look at. When it has just finished 'swirling', pour it off gradually into another pail—the thick gritty part of the whiting will have

HORSEBANE
(Oenanthe Phellandrium)

already been left in the first pail. Empty this out and 'swirl' the liquid a second time, repeating, as before, the pouring off into the first pail. Now let the balance settle down until the liquid clears. You will find the 'whiting' has settled at the bottom, and the water will be nearly clear. Drain the water off gently and then the wet whiting should be laid on a newspaper in the sun to dry. This will now be 'soft and silky'. Add to this half an ounce of rouge powder. Mix together and you've got the finest plate powder in the world— 15s. worth at a cost of 3d. Usually the fakers leave out the rouge (they think it's too expensive).

A few other recipes that you will enjoy reading about and perhaps find useful are the following:

EVERBRITE LACQUER FOR ALL BRASS PLATES, ETC.

This can be made very simply, but it is a wonderful lacquer. Get from the chemist (or, better still, the oil and colour shop) a quarter of a pint of amylacetate (it smells like pear-drops). Add a piece of clean celluloid (from a broken windscreen or an accumulator), stir it up after it has stood for a day, and it is ready for use. *Keep airtight.* Next clean the metal which is to be treated, making sure you have left no remains of the polish, or powder, on it. Then, with a nice soft brush, paint over with the lacquer. The lacquer dries nearly instantaneously and the article coated will not tarnish for months. When you want to remove the old lacquer, add new lacquer and wipe it off very quickly. Then re-coat again with your brush, as in the first instance.

ENGLISH ELM
(Ulmus Campestris, Nettle Family)

THE MAGIC CARPET-CLEANER

Get one pound of Castile soap. Cut it up and add one pint of water and a drop of liquid ammonia. Boil up for a few minutes until the soap has melted, then place the substance into tins or jars. This is the thing that has such 'magic cleaning effects' on white kid gloves and felt hats, carpets, rugs, etc. But don't expect to get the dirt off as quickly as the 'workers' do it, as yours will be 'naturally' dirtied. Theirs is a 'fake' soil.

SILVER-PLATING ARTICLES

Mix two ounces of nitric acid with half an ounce of mercury (quicksilver). Drop into the solution any little old pieces of silver that you may have about, such as broken silver brooches or pins, etc. The acid will quickly 'eat' them away. Now add four ounces of *boiled* water to the above, and, with an old toothbrush for preference, brush the liquid on to any old brass or metal articles. They will be 'plated like lightning'. Now, again, don't think they will remain like it for ever; they won't. It's just one of the many 'fakes' that you can easily be 'took in' over. But if you want to make a real good temporary show this recipe is useful.

SOAP

Soap plays a prominent part in many of the faker's stock-in-trade, and I have seen it sold in many ways, from 'corn cures' to preventing steam on your eye-glasses. For this last purpose it is marvellous. Just

NUTMEG
(Myristica Fragrans)

try it. Rub a bit of soap on your eyeglass lens, and then with a dry cloth rub it off. You will find a beautiful polish, and if you breathe on the glass you will find it will not 'blur'. If, after cleaning a piece of glass in this manner, you hold it over the steam of a kettle, it will still remain clear. It looks wonderful when you see it demonstrated.

SPIRIT WRITING (NO. 1)

Write with a new nib (or one that will not corrode), using a solution of sulphate of copper, on ordinary paper. Then let the papers dry thoroughly. To make the writing appear place them in a tin containing 'block' ammonia or in a jar with liquid ammonia. If using liquid ammonia, the jar must have a rest to lay the papers on to prevent their getting damp. Great fun can be had at Christmas parties by writing out the 'fortunes' of the different guests.

SPIRIT WRITING (NO. 2)

Squeeze the juice from a lemon and with a very clean pen, or, better still, a pointed piece of wood, write on the papers. Simply by holding the papers to the heat of the fire the 'magic' writing will appear.

BITTER SWEET
(Amara Dulcis, Solanum Dulcamara,
Potato Family)

ASPARAGUS
(Asparagus Officinalis—Lily Family)

CLEAVERS

APPENDIX

I have mentioned various herbs, flowers, roots, and barks which can usually be grown in one's own garden or found in the lanes and by-ways. The following lists include those I have already mentioned and some others besides. The method of use is the same in every case: infuse one ounce of the herb, root, or flower in one pint of water, and take a wineglassful night and morning. Here are the names and the uses to which they can be put.

BARKS:
Alder	-	-	- Aperient.
Ash	-	-	- Laxative.
Birch	-	-	- Eczema.
Cherry	-	-	- Lung Diseases.
Oak	-	-	- Antiseptic and Tonic.
Willow	-	-	- Rheumatic Fever.

FLOWERS:
Camomile	-	- Hysteria.
Elder	-	- Urinary troubles.
Hop	-	- Stomach complaints.
Marigold	-	- Promotes Perspiration.
Red Clover	-	- Coughs.
Safflower	-	- Fevers and Female complaints.

ROOTS:
Dandelion	-	- Rheumatics and Liver.
Lily of Valley	-	- Valvular Disease of Heart.
Male Fern	-	- Worms.
Marshmallow	-	- Dysentery.
Red Dock	-	- Purifier of the Blood.
Rhubarb	-	- Aperient.
Solomon's Seal	-	- Pulmonary troubles.

AMERICAN COWSLIP
(Caltha Palustrus—Crowfoot Family)

HERBS:

Ash leaves	- Rheumatoid Arthritis.
Blackberry	- Diarrhoea.
Black Currant	- Sore Throats, Catarrh.
Camomile	- Debility
Dandelion	- Laxative and Tonic.
Golden Rod	- Correct Vomiting.
Ground Ivy	- Internal Ulcers.
Horehound	- Coughs, and for making Beer.
Iceland Moss	- Appetizer.
Lobelia	- Bronchial complaints and Croup.
Nettles	- Blood-pressure and Rash.
Peppermint	- Flatulence
Plantain	- Piles.
Raspberry	- Gargle for Throat.
Rosemary	- Hair stimulant.
Scabious	- Internal Inflammation.
Sorrel	- A cooling Fever drink.
Southernwood	- Female disorders.
Thyme	- An Antiseptic.
Violet*	- Poultices.
(Wood) Sage	- Kidneys, Liver.
Wormwood	- Digestion, Worms in Children.
Yarrow	- Colds and Fevers.

A few of the things mentioned are useful for many complaints. One such is *isinglass*, which is obtained from the swimming bladders of various species of acipenser and is prepared and finely shredded. This is sold in various forms under fancy names at high prices. Use it in cases of sleeplessness, brain fatigue, and nervous troubles. It is also good for children suffering from rickets and young persons

* See page vii.

COMFREY
(Symphytum Officinale, Borage Family)

using a lot of energy in study. The gipsy makes his own
'brain food', those travelling in Rumania, Hungary, and
Russia using the bladder of the sturgeon. But when you
buy this ask for 'Brazilian' isinglass. Rub a little up and
place in a glass of hot milk (an ounce will make about
thirty doses). Take it the last thing at night before retiring
to bed.

CORIANDER
(Coriander Sativum, Parsley Family)

NOTES AND RECIPES

MANDRAKE
(Podophyllum Peltatum, Barberry Family)

FLAX

NOTES AND RECIPES

MANNA TREE
(Fraxinus Ornus—Olive Family)

MISTLETOE

KEN BISHOP